Cover illustration: Although obsolescent by the close of the Second World War, the Sherman gave yeoman service under the particular and peculiar conditions pertaining in Korea, and it remained the most numerous Allied tank throughout the conflict. (US Army)

1. With its tracks and suspension well protected against artillery fire, 'Becher's Brook', a Centurion Mk. III of B Squadron, 5th Royal Inniskilling Dragoon Guards, engages enemy positions during December 1952. Note the small-arms ammunition boxes and field telephones on the rear top of the turret. (5RIDG)

TANKS ILLUSTRATED NO.14

Tank War Korea

SIMON DUNSTAN

a&ap
ARMS AND ARMOUR PRESS
London – Melbourne – Harrisburg, Pa. – Cape Town

TK45

Introduction

Published in 1985 by Arms and Armour Press, Lionel Leventhal Limited, 2-6 Hampstead High Street, London NW3 1QQ; 11 Munro Street, Port Melbourne 3207, Australia; Sanso Centre, 8 Adderley Street, P.O. Box 94, Cape Town 8000; Cameron and Kelker Streets, P.O. Box 1831, Harrisburg, Pennsylvania 17105, USA

British Library Cataloguing in Publication Data:
Dunstan, Simon
Tank war Korea.—(Tanks illustrated 14)
1. United States. *Army*—Armoured troops
2. United Nations. *Emergency Force*
3. Korean War, 1950-1953—Tank warfare
I. Title II. Series
951.9′042 DS918
ISBN 0-85368-682-3

Edited and laid out by Roger Chesneau.
Printed in Italy
by Tipolitografia G. Canale & C. S.p.A. - Turin
in association with Keats European Ltd.

To W. and J.G.

◀2
2. The classic image of the Tiger schemes adopted by tank crews for Operations 'Killer' and 'Ripper', the UN counteroffensive of March and April 1951. This M4A3(76)W HVSS is preparing to advance along the Han river area during an attack by the 5th Regimental Combat Team, 18 February 1951. (US Army)

With the possible exception of certain terrain encountered during the Italian campaign of the Second World War, there can be few regions less suited to the employment of tanks than the far peninsula of Korea, traversed as it is by innumerable ranges of steep hills with intervening rice paddy fields often deep in water. Indeed, before the outbreak of hostilities, American military advisers to the Republic of Korea (ROK) discounted the possibility of an armoured onslaught through such mountainous landscape, and so the ROK Army had neither adequate anti-tank weapons nor AFVs. As a result, when the North Korean People's Army (NKPA) attacked across the 38th Parallel on 25 June 1950 with only 150 T-34/85s, the ROK Army was broken within days.

The United States quickly came to the aid of the stricken republic and galvanized the United Nations into condemning and countering such unprovoked aggression. Even so, with only limited resources in this erstwhile backwater of world politics, the unprepared US Army units drawn from occupation duties in Japan were forced back into an ever-shrinking enclave around the southern port of Pusan and were hard pressed to contain the Communist offensive. However, under the dynamic and forceful direction of General Douglas MacArthur, the Commander-in-Chief United Nations Command, and with an immense influx of men and material from the USA, the situation was reversed and the NKPA was defeated on the battlefield, the remnants being pursued to the border of that hitherto sleeping giant, China. The latter's reaction was swift and massive, and thirty divisions fell upon the United Nations forces, which retreated once more below the 38th Parallel.

Throughout this mobile phase of the war, tanks played a prominent part in both offensive and defensive operations, but by the end of 1951 the campaign had become somewhat static, a condition which prevailed for nearly two years while protracted truce negotiations were conducted at Panmunjon. During this period tanks were dug into prepared positions on commanding sites with wide fields of fire and were employed as fixed direct-fire artillery in close support of the infantry. On occasions tank raids were launched into No Man's Land against enemy positions, but they were rarely successful and the risk of losing tanks (more often because of the appalling terrain than to enemy action) was disproportionate to the results that might be achieved.

As indicated in the captions, the majority of the photographs are reproduced by courtesy of the United States Army and United States Marine Corps, to whom I extend my thanks for their co-operation. In addition, I wish to acknowledge the assistance of the military attaché at the South Korean Embassy in London, *Soldier* Magazine and the National Army Museum, Chelsea, as well as those individuals who kindly provided photographs from their private collections, in particular Lt. Col. George Forty RTR (Ret) and Col. Peter Massy RTR (Ret).

Simon Dunstan

▲3

3. On 25 June 1950 the North Korean People's Army (NKPA) invaded the Republic of Korea (ROK) across the 38th Parallel. In the van were the T-34/85s of 105th Armoured Brigade, comprising three tank regiments each of 40 tanks. First formed in Sa-dong as the 115th Tank Regiment in May 1947, the unit was reorganized into the 105th Armoured Brigade on 16 May 1949. This tank brigade was a unit of which the North Korean rulers were particularly proud, nicknaming it 'Tiger's Cave Sadong Unit'. (ROK Army)

4. Against the ill-equipped ROK Army, the T-34/85s swept all before them, and within three days the South Korean capital, Seoul, had fallen. The photograph shows tanks and infantry fighting their way into the city, which the original North Korean caption declared was 'the den of the US imperialist aggressors and their lackeys'. In recognition of the part it played in capturing the city, the 105th Armoured Brigade was raised to division status and became known as the 'Seoul Division'. (ROK Army)

▼4

5▲

5. Crew members pose in front of their M24 Chaffee 'Rebel's Roost', which is credited as being the first American tank to see action in Korea. On 10 July 1950 three M24s of the 24th Infantry Division fought a delaying action at Chonui against a powerful force of T-34/85s. In an unequal contest, two Chaffees were lost, but not before one T-34 was destroyed. (US Army)

6. In addition to the tanks of the 105th Armoured Brigade, the NKPA deployed several battalions of SU76 self-propelled guns, a total of 176 such weapons being committed in the early battles. The only other NKPA AFV to be used was the BA64 armoured car, which equipped the 303rd Mobile Reconnaissance Unit, although only in small numbers since the majority of its personnel were mounted on 'Motorjik' motorcycle-sidecar combinations. (ROK Army)

6▼

▲7

▲8

9▶

7. By late July, the United Nations forces had been driven back into a pocket around the southern port of Pusan, but during August six US tank battalions arrived in Korea to bolster the shrinking perimeter. Several fierce tank battles occurred, in particular on the Taegu-Sangju road, which became known as the 'Bowling Alley' after repeated attacks by NKPA armour. Here, an M26 Pershing of the 73rd Tank Battalion engages an NKPA party laying mines in the 'Bowling Alley' on 24 August. (US Army)

8. Troops of the 9th Infantry Regiment, 2nd Infantry Division, with attached ROK soldiers, move out on the back of an M26 Pershing to meet a North Korean probe across the Naktong river on 3 September 1950. By this time the perimeter had been consolidated and the UN forces were able to launch limited counterattacks against the enemy. (US Army)

9. In a masterly counterstroke to envelop the over-extended NKPA from the rear, an amphibious assault was unleashed on 15 September against Inchon, the port closest to Seoul. Crewmen of Company A, 1st Marine Tank Battalion, are seen here loading their M26 Pershings with 90mm ammunition on board a landing craft bound for Inchon. On the glacis plate of the nearest M26 is a kill tally of three T-34s; this Pershing, of 3 Platoon, 'Able' Company, fought a decisive action at Obong-Ni ridge on 17 August in which four T-34/85s were destroyed. (USMC)

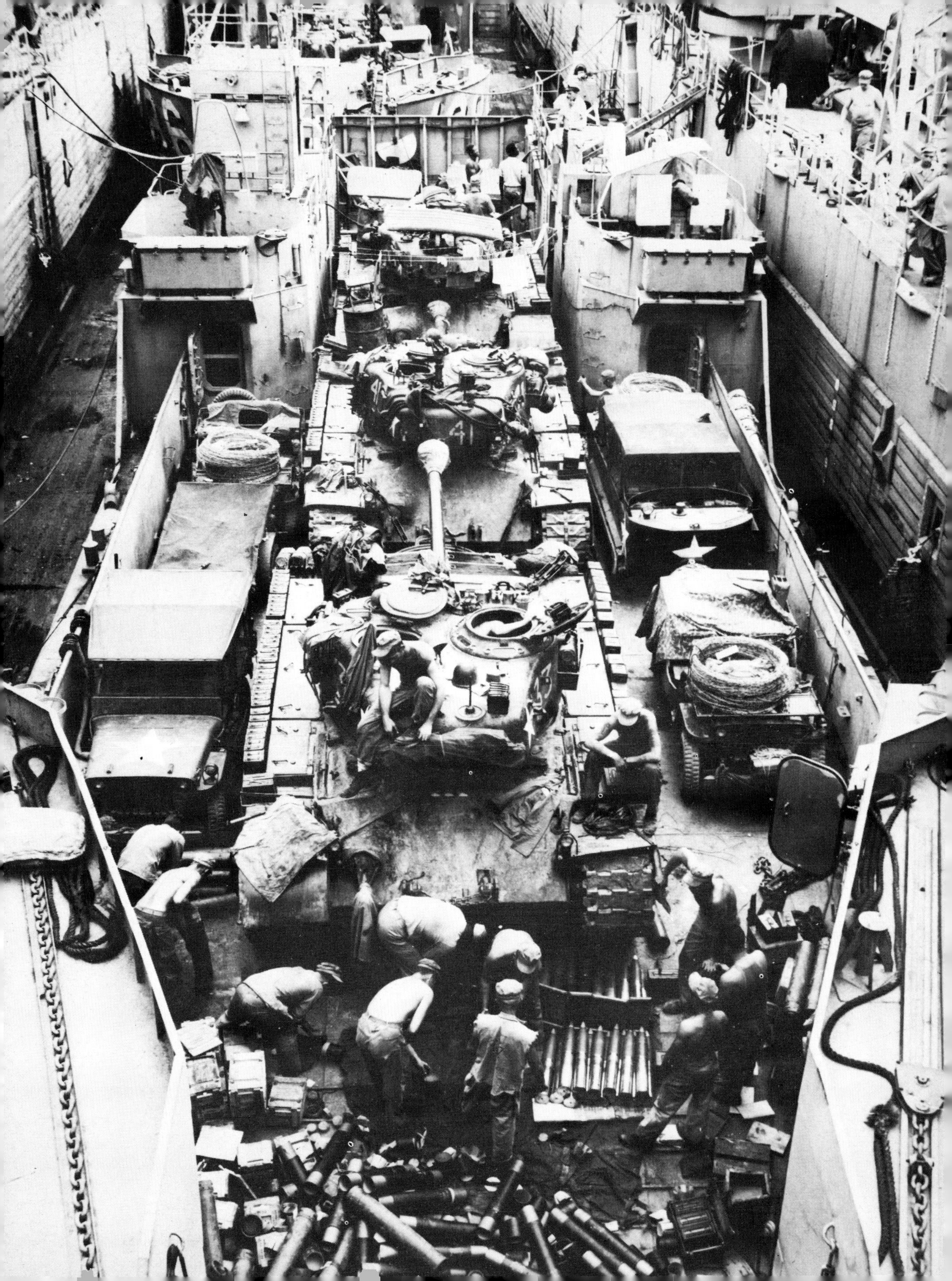

▲10

10. LVT-3 amtracs (amphibious tractors) of the 1st Marine Amphibian Tractor Battalion carrying riflemen of 3/5 Marines churn towards Wolmi-Do island – the first objective during the Inchon landings – at the outset of the assault. (US Army)

11. In conjunction with the Inchon landings, the UN forces launched a major counteroffensive to break out of the Pusan perimeter. Here, M45s of the 6th Tank Battalion, 24th Infantry Division, negotiate the Kumho river on an underwater crossing of rocks and sandbags reinforcing the river bed. The M45 was a close-support version of the M26 Pershing armed with a 105mm howitzer M4 in an 8in thick mantlet. (US Army)

▼11

12▲

12. An M4A3 HVSS (Horizontal Volute Spring Suspension) POA-CWS-H5 flame-thrower of the 1st Marine Tank Battalion rolls through the outskirts of Yongdongpo during the advance on Seoul. The flame projector is mounted in the mantlet next to the 105mm howitzer, with its fuel tanks inside the hull. The Marines initially deployed fifty flame tanks to Korea. (USMC)

13. On 20 September 1950, 5th Marine Regiment launched an attack across the Han river, mounted in amtracs of the 1st Marine Amphibian Tractor Battalion. These amtracs are the LVT3(C) model – a post-Second World War modification to the standard vehicle incorporating hatches over the troop compartment and a gunshield for the .50 calibre Browning. (USMC)

13▼

▲14

▲15 ▼16

14. Five days later, the Marines broke into Seoul against extremely fierce resistance. An M26 Pershing of 1 Platoon, Company B, 1st Marine Tank Battalion, pushes forward along a bullet-swept street with pictures of Communist leaders Stalin and Kim Il-Sung hanging in the background. On 27 September the city fell to the Marines. (USMC)
15. An M29C Weasel climbs the 'bund' of a rice paddy field as it lays field telephone cable in the Hungnam area in November 1950. On account of its low weight and high flotation, the Weasel proved to be a very successful cargo carrier in the boggy and mountainous Korean terrain. (USMC)
16. After the capture of Seoul, the UN forces pursued the stricken NKPA into North Korea, and by the end of November advance units had reached the Yalu river on the border of the People's Republic of China. Laden with troops, an M26 Pershing is shown here negotiating an icy river during the push northwards. (US Army)
17. With UN troops nearing their frontier, the Chinese Communist Forces (CCF) struck back in strength with over thirty divisions; fearing envelopment, the Eighth Army and the X Corps fell back. An M40 155mm Gun Motor Carriage of the 937th Field Artillery Battalion here fires on enemy positions on the Central Korean front. (US Army)
18. An M4A3 105mm Howitzer HVSS tankdozer with M1A1 blade scrapes a track near Hamhung; the vehicle is attached to Company B, 1st Marine Tank Battalion. Tankdozers were vital to the maintenance of the marginal Korean roads and to the preparation of new ones. (USMC)
19. M4A3(76)W HVSS Shermans of the 89th Tank Battalion carrying men of the 27th Infantry Regiment, 25th Infantry Division, retire to the south bank of the Han river after evacuating Seoul, January 1951. UN forces retreated some 150 miles before the Chinese offensive was contained by the end of January. (US Army)

17▲

18▲ 19▼

▲20 ▼21

22▲

20. After their epic battle at the Chosin Reservoir, members of the Headquarters and Service Company, 2nd Battalion, 7th Marines, board LVTs at Hungnam for their journey to troopships in the harbour. These amtracs of Company B, 1st Marine Amphibian Tractor Battalion, are LVT3s except the one in the foreground which is an LVT3(C). (USMC)
21. An M4A3 105mm Howitzer HVSS tankdozer leads M26 Pershings and a TRV (Tank Recovery Vehicle) of the 1st Marine Tank Battalion across a paddy field in the Pohang area. (US Army)
22. Empty shell cases are discarded from an M24 after a fire mission against Communist forces near Wonju, February 1951. After the 1950 Communist offensive, NKPA armour did not reappear on the battlefield in significant numbers and the M24 Chaffee, once again, proved its effectiveness as a fire support vehicle in difficult terrain on account of its light weight and manoeuvrability. The crewman on the engine decks would man the .50 calibre Browning mounted at the rear of the turret should the occasion demand. (US Army)
23. Resplendent in the full Tiger colour scheme, M46 Pattons of the 6th Tank Battalion form up in firing positions during an action against Chinese forces, 6 March 1951. These colour schemes were adopted in order to instil terror in the supposedly superstitious Communists at the time of the Chinese New Year marking the end of the Year of the Tiger. (US Army)

23▼

▲24

24. M4A3(76)W HVSS Shermans of Company C ('Rice's Red Devils'), 89th Tank Battalion, cross the Han river in an attack against Communist positions during Operation 'Ripper' in March 1951. This particular unit created its own colour scheme of devil faces on the glacis plates of its tanks. (US Army)

25. M26 Pershings and an M4A3 105mm Howitzer HVSS tankdozer (without its blade) of Company C, 1st Marine Tank Battalion, engage enemy bunkers on a hillside near Hongchon on 15 March 1951. Typically during the mobile phase of the war, the enemy holds the hilltops while the UN forces dominate the valleys and roads. (USMC)

26. An M41 Howitzer Motor Carriage of Battery 'A', 92nd Armored Field Artillery Battalion (SP155), is loaded during a fire mission in support of the 1st Marine Division on 24 April 1951. Minutes after this photograph was taken the battalion position was attacked by Chinese infantry and after a desperate struggle the assault was repulsed, 179 of the enemy being killed at a cost of four dead and eleven wounded. The 92nd adopted the nickname 'Red Devils', as the cartoons on the vehicle hull sides and crew helmets emphasize. (US Army)

27. Members of the Heavy Mortar Company, 9th Infantry Regiment, are moved to the front line aboard an M39 Armored Utility Vehicle of the 2nd Reconnaissance Company, 2nd 'Indianhead' Infantry Division, March 1951. The M39 was based on the chassis of the M18 Hellcat tank destroyer. (US Army)

▼25

26▲ 27▼

▲28 ▼29

30▲

28. The gun crew of an M41 155mm self-propelled howitzer of the 999th Armored Field Artillery Battalion (SP155), attached to the 24th Infantry Division, prepare their vehicles before going into action in support of the 19th Infantry Regiment near Yangpyung in March 1951. Note that the national white star has been subdued to avoid presenting an aiming mark for enemy gunners. (US Army)
29. The poor roads preventing them from accompanying the infantry, M4A3(76)W HVSS Shermans of the 17th Tank Company, 17th Regimental Combat Team of 7th Infantry Division, support an attack at Pangnim by firing as artillery batteries – a commonplace role for tanks during the Korean War. Note the stacks of ammunition boxes behind the Shermans and the piles of rounds on their engine decks. (US Army)
30. Perched on a narrow ridgeline, M24 Chaffees lash out at the enemy as a water-cooled .30 calibre Browning machine gun is employed in the sustained-fire role in the foreground. Note that the loader of the nearest Chaffee is using an M1919A4 .30 calibre Browning mounted forward of his hatch so that he can fire to the front without exposing himself – a sensible precaution not possible with the .50 calibre Browning at the turret rear. (US Army)
31. A pair of M24 Chaffees of the 25th Reconnaissance Company returns from a patrol behind enemy lines along a railway track north of the Han river. These Chaffees display impressive Dragon colour schemes over the glacis plates and turret fronts. The .50 calibre Brownings have been moved forward of the commander's hatch for greater flexibility. (US Army)

31▼

▲32

32. An M4A3(76)W HVSS Sherman is winched aboard an M15 Semitrailer near the front lines of the 25th Infantry Division north of the Han river. The complete rig is the 40-ton tank recovery truck-trailer M25 with M15 Semitrailer and armoured Truck-Tractor M26. It could recover and transport damaged tanks weighing up to 80,000lb. (US Army)

33. A graphic example of the problems of armoured combat in Korea: an M46 Patton of the 6th Tank Battalion tows to safety a bogged companion that has slipped off the primitive track into the mire of a rice paddy field. (US Army)

▼33

34▲

34. An aged Korean mama-san strolls along oblivious to her surroundings as a late-production M32B1 Tank Recovery Vehicle prepares to tow an M46 Patton, stranded in heavy sand, from the battle zone to a rear-area ordnance depot for repairs. (US Army)

35. Machine gunners on an M3A1 Half-Track of the 15th Anti-aircraft Artillery Automatic Weapons Battalion (SP), 7th Infantry Division, return fire during an action against Communist forces on the outskirts of Yanggu, 15 April 1951. Half-track vehicles were used extensively throughout the Korean War both as armoured personnel carriers and as general load carriers. (US Army)

35▼

▲36 ▼37

36. An M7B1 Howitzer Motor Carriage (named 'Belchin' Bitch') of the 937th Field Artillery Battalion crosses a pontoon bridge during an operation in support of the 1st Marine Division, 16 April 1951. Without the prodigious efforts of the engineers, the heavily mechanized UN forces would have been rendered immobile. (US Army)

37. 'Longtom' M40 155mm Gun Motor Carriages of the 204th Field Artillery Battalion blast away at Communist forces north of Seoul during the Chinese Spring Offensive, 29 April 1951. The massive firepower of UN aircraft and artillery did much to blunt the overwhelming manpower advantage of the CCF and NKPA. (US Army)

38. A mortar crew of the 19th Infantry Regiment, 24th Infantry Division, advances behind an M39 Armored Utility Vehicle, mounting quadruple .50 calibre machine guns, near the village of Maeng-dong, 20 May 1951. A number of M39s were converted to self-propelled carriers for weapons such as the M55 or 81mm mortar. (US Army)

39. M24 Chaffees of the Reconnaissance Company of the 1st Cavalry Division cross the Imjin river over a pontoon bridge, 6 June 1951. Note the wire frame along the sides acting as a stowage basket for the crew's kit and ammunition boxes. (US Army)

40. M4A3(76)W HVSS Shermans of the 70th Tank Battalion attached to the 1st US Cavalry Division ford the Imjin as they move out on patrol north of the river. Although not readily apparent in the photograph, these Shermans are each decorated with a tiger's head and splayed claws on the glacis plate – characteristic of this unit during the spring of 1951. (US Army)

38▲

39▲ 40▼

▲41

41. 'Eagle Claw', an M24 Chaffee of the 3rd Reconnaissance Company, 3rd Infantry Division, fires on a group of Chinese soldiers encountered while on patrol near Songbong-dong, 20 May 1951. By this time most crews had mounted the .50 calibre M2HB Browning forward of the turret between the two crew hatches so that either the loader or the commander could fire the weapon forward. (US Army)

42. Shermans of the 17th Regimental Combat Team, 7th Infantry Division, move off to assault Chinese positions near Hwach-on. Although the correct designation for this model of Sherman is M4A3(76)W HVSS, tank crews still called them 'Easy Eights', which derived from the Second World War experimental nomenclature of M4A3E8. (US Army)

43. South Korean ammunition porters trudge along the roadside as an M7B1 105mm Howitzer Motor Carriage thunders past towards Yong Pong. To facilitate high-angle indirect fire among the steep hills of Korea, a number of these vehicles were modified during the war by raising the howitzer mounting in order to increase the maximum elevation of the 105mm; such vehicles were designated M7B2. (US Army)

44. Mounted on earth ramps to increase maximum elevation, M4A3(76)W HVSS Shermans of the 23rd Tank Company of the 'Indianhead' Division support an infantry attack against CCF positions north of Pia-ri on the East Central front, 18 September 1951. The vertical surfaces of these tanks are painted with irregular earth brown stripes – a fairly common camouflage scheme during the summer months. (US Army)

▼42

43▲ 44▼

45. Ploughing through deep mud, an M16 Multiple Gun Motor Carriage of the 15th Anti-aircraft Artillery Automatic Weapons Battalion (SP), 7th Infantry Division, bypasses a cratered road while moving to the front line during Operation 'Cleaver' against the CCF south of Kumsong, 21 September 1951. The primary mission of these vehicles was air defence, but in Korea they were predominantly employed in fire support to the infantry. (US Army)
46. An M4A3(76)W HVSS Sherman of Bravo Company, 89th Tank Battalion, 25th Infantry Division, gives fire support to the assault platoon of Company A, 1st Battalion, 35th Infantry Regiment, during an attack on a hill near Kumhwa in September 1951. Note the company, unit and division code on the rear hull-plate. (US Army)
47. Surrounded by empty ammunition boxes, the 'quad fifties' of these M16s of the 26th Anti-aircraft Artillery Automatic Weapons Battalion (SP) lay down supporting fire for Company A, 19th Infantry Regiment, 24th Infantry Division, near Chip-o-ri, 14 October 1951. Although unsuited to the close-support role on account of its thin armour, the M16 was devastating against the 'human wave' tactics of the CCF, fully justifying its nickname of the 'Grinder' or 'Meat-Chopper'. (US Army)
48. Tank crewmen of 1st Marine Tank Battalion replenish their M46 Patton with 90mm main-armament ammunition between missions in the fire support role, November 1951. This photograph clearly shows the revised engine decks of the M46, as compared to the M26, with the exhausts mounted on the fenders. (USMC)

▲45 ▼46

47▲ 48▼

26
26

49. Cargo nets are unloaded from the ship *Belgium Victory* into a versatile 'Duck' (DUKW) at Inchon harbour, November 1951. The GMC 2½-ton 6×6 Amphibian Truck soldiered on through the Korean War, plying its trade between ships and shore where port facilities proved inadequate for the massive flow of military material. (US Army)

50. Bone-chilling wind was the common enemy through the winters of the Korean campaign. Here, an infantryman stands guard on an M16 of the 21st AAA AW Bn (SP), 25th Infantry Division, south-east of Pyongyang, 23 November 1951. In the background is a smoking petrol space heater – the cause of almost as many casualties as combat during the depths of winter. (US Army)

51. 'Bulldog's Bark', an M40 of Battery B, 937th Field Artillery Battalion, lights up the night sky as it pounds Communist positions during a fire mission in support of the 25th Infantry Division near the village of Munema, 25 November 1951. (US Army)

52. An M32A1B3 of 'Dog' Company, 1st Marine Tank Battalion, lifts an M1A1 dozerblade assembly as its parent vehicle, an M4A3 (105) HVSS tankdozer, reverses underneath for attachment to the mountings outboard of the horizontal volute spring suspension. (USMC)

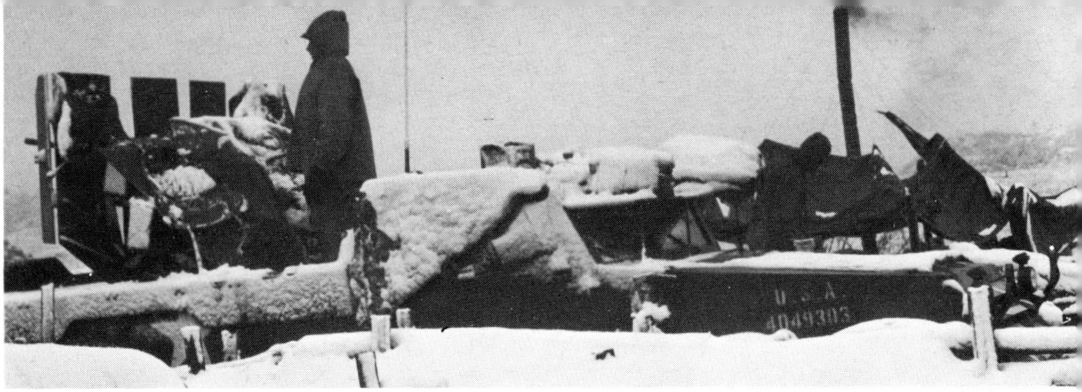

50▲

51▲ 52▼

◀49

▲53

53. 'Ridgerunning', an M46 Patton of the 6th Tank Battalion, negotiates a track bulldozed across the ridge of Hill 663 south of Kumsong as it fires in support of Company C, 19th Infantry Regiment, 24th Infantry Division, on 13 December 1951. (US Army)
54. Members of the 6th Tank Battalion survey the approaches to the Kumsong valley from atop their M46 Patton, 13 January 1952. The rigours of the cold demanded meticulous maintenance of tanks and vehicles – tracks, batteries, cooling system – since the failure of any component could lead to a vehicle being stranded in hostile terrain. (US Army)
55. Two Marine tankmen warm their hands in the exhaust of their M46 Patton. (USMC)
56. A Marine flame-throwing tank (POA-CWS-H5) lumbers along a ridgeline in search of enemy snipers. The slightest mistake in steering could cause a tank to plunge down a hillside, often for hundreds of feet. (USMC)

▼54

55▲ 56▼

▲57 ▼58

59▲

57. A US Marine Corps command and communication tank acts as a relay station in an orchard south-east of the truce conference site at Panmunjom. The tank is fitted with a dummy gun and extra radios, together with the array of antennae which gave rise to the vehicle's nickname of 'Porcupine'. (USMC)

58. US Army M4A3(76)W HVSS Shermans support Marine infantrymen in an attack on simulated enemy positions during training on the Kimpo peninsula, 4 June 1952. Despite the introduction of the M46 Patton, the 'Easy Eight' Sherman remained the most numerous Allied tank throughout the war. (USMC)

59. 'Bouncing Betsy', an M39 Armored Utility Vehicle of the 45th Reconnaissance Company, 45th Infantry Division, returns to the MLR (Main Line of Resistance) after delivering supplies and equipment to a forward outpost during the fighting west of Chorwon, 6 July 1952 – a task typical for the Buick M39. (US Army)

60. To enable tanks to be recovered under hostile fire without exposing crew members, the Marines developed an automatic coupling device to hook on to a disabled tank. The hook is shown on the right-hand vehicle, and to the left is the coupling device (which was normally fitted to a Tank Recovery Vehicle). (USMC)

60▼

33AA
B-251

61. The crew of an M19 Gun Carriage of Battery B, 3rd Anti-aircraft Artillery Automatic Weapons Battalion (SP), 3rd Infantry Division, pose atop their vehicle, August 1952. The twin 40mm Bofors-armed M19 was commonly employed in conjunction with the M16 'quad fifty'. Note the spare 40mm barrels laid across the engine decks and the M12 body armour draped over the side of the fighting compartment. (US Army)

62. Employing an M29C Weasel to overcome the heavy mud, Marines clad in M1951 flak vests move ammunition and supplies up to the front lines for units of the 1st Marine Division during the battle for 'Bunker Hill'. Typically for Weasels, the bow plate is raised to aid driver vision, exposing a 3.5in rocket launcher. (USMC)
63. Redlegs of Battery A, 17th Field Artillery Battalion, fire an M43 8in Howitzer Motor Carriage at Communist-held positions as they provide fire support for advancing troops of the 2nd Infantry Division on 'Old Baldy', 22 August 1952. The M43 was a particularly potent weapon against Communist entrenched positions and field fortifications. (US Army)

62▶

▼63

64▲

◀65

64. An M46 Patton of the 1st Marine Tank Battalion tows a 3in Anti-Tank Gun M5 to a new fire position during September 1952. Note the exposed infantry phone on the rear plate of the M46 and the Marines standing to either side wearing the newly introduced fragmentation vest body armour. (USMC)

65. M4A3(76)W HVSS Shermans of the 4th Platoon, Company A, 89th Tank Battalion, 25th Infantry Division, fire on Chinese positions in the hills overlooking the Satae-ni valley. Note the expended shell cases beside the tank and the three-colour camouflage scheme. The heavy consumption of ammunition during such fire missions resulted in rapid barrel and trunnion wear. (US Army)

▲66

▲67 ▼68

66. During the static phase of the war both sides built elaborate field fortifications as protection from the elements and artillery fire. Here, members of the Korean Service Corps unload beams from an M39 Armored Utility Vehicle at the 2nd Infantry Division supply point on 'Old Baldy' near Chorwon. The beams are used in the construction of prefabricated bunkers. Note that the M39 in the background has shed a track – a frequent occurrence for all AFVs operating in the rugged hills of Korea. (US Army)

67. Sporting a winter camouflage scheme of white stripes over olive drab, two M46 Pattons of the 64th Tank Battalion, 3rd Infantry Division, guard a road out of the gutted city of Chorwon, 6 February 1953. Note the small compensating idler between the rear sprocket and the first roadwheel – a further identifying feature of the M46. (US Army)

68. When perched on their hilltop fire positions, tanks were occasionally exposed to sneak attacks by enemy bazooka teams. As a counter to this threat some tanks, such as this M46 Patton of 'Dog' Company, 1st Marine Tank Battalion, were fitted with a wire-frame cage around the turret in order to detonate the 3.5in rockets before they struck the armour itself. Note the searchlight mounted above the barrel of the M46 in the background. (USMC)

69. Tank recovery vehicles were essential to aid mobility and retrieve disabled vehicles of armoured units operating in the hostile terrain of Korea. This M32A1B3 TRV was attached to the 1st Armored Amphibious Tractor Battalion operating on the Kimpo peninsula. (USMC)
70. During the final months of the war, the Communists launched concerted attacks against certain key Allied positions in order to gain concessions at the truce talks at Panmunjon. One of the fiercest actions was at Pork Chop Hill, an isolated position forward of the 7th Infantry Division MLR. Cruelly exposed to mortar and artillery fire, the 'Chop' could only be supplied and casualties could only be evacuated by AFVs. Here, medical corpsmen unload wounded troops from an M39 of the Armored Personnel Carrier Platoon (Provisional) returning from Pork Chop Hill, 17 April 1953. (US Army)

69▲ 70▼

▲71

▲72 ▼73

71. The first British tank unit to serve in Korea was C Squadron, 7th Royal Tank Regiment, equipped with Churchill Crocodile flame-throwers. Disembarking at Pusan on 15 November 1950, the squadron was attached to the 29th Infantry Brigade Group and moved northwards by train to join the UN advance into North Korea. Owing to a lack of railway stock, one troop travelled by road, covering 200 miles on its tracks to establish a march record for Churchills; here, the troop motors through Seoul on its journey northwards – the Crocodile flame trailers were discarded at an early stage. The leading Churchill Mk. VII is named 'Genie' on the air louvres; all tanks in 7RTR had names beginning with the seventh letter of the alphabet. (*Soldier*)

72. On 15 November 1950, the 8th King's Royal Irish Hussars (8KRIH) also arrived at Pusan. The Regiment was equipped with three sabre squadrons of Centurions Mk. III and a reconnaissance troop of Cromwells Mk. VII as well as supporting vehicles including Churchill ARVs and Bridgelayers; one of the last-mentioned vehicles is seen on a railway flatcar during the journey northwards. The first 'tank train' arrived at the North Korean capital of Pyongyang on 30 November. Lashed down by plaited rice straw ropes, the tanks far exceeded the loading gauge of the rolling stock, which bowed ominously under the weight, and the slow wood-burning train took seven days and nights to reach Pyongyang. With rations for only four days, the tanks crews were obliged to expropriate American provisions from boxcars en route. (Private Collection)

73, 74. On 2 December, with the tanks still on the rails, came news of a heavy defeat north of Pyongyang. The Centurions of A Squadron plus one troop of C Squadron were hastily unloaded and took up positions on the western outskirts of the city. The C Squadron troop was given the task of guarding the crossing on the north bank of the Taedong river. In these photographs, a Centurion Mk. III covers the withdrawal of UN troops through Pyongyang, 3 December. The plate on the turret stowage bin indicates that it is the troop sergeant's tank of 1 Troop, C Squadron. (US Army)

75. With the Chinese advancing rapidly, the Centurions of the 8th Hussars were ordered to withdraw to prevent the top-secret tanks from falling into enemy hands. After a perilous trip southwards in the freezing cold, Centurions Mk. III are here seen pulling back through the streets of Seoul during the retreat of the UN forces to a line on the south bank of the Han river. (*Soldier*)

74▲ 75▼

▲76 ▼77

76. 'Cracador', a Centaur Dozer, prepares defensive positions on a featureless snow-bound island in the Han river for the Centurions of C Squadron covering the escape route of the 29th Brigade, which would defend Seoul while the 25th US Infantry Division and the 1st ROK division withdrew through them over the remaining bridges. (US Army)
77. After the withdrawal of the Centurions to Suwon and Pusan, one element of 8KRIH – 'Cooper Force' – remained north of the Han river in support of 29th Brigade. 'Cooper Force' comprised the six Cromwells of the Reconnaissance Troop reinforced by eight Gunner OP Cromwells of the 45th Field Regiment (Royal Artillery) and was so named after the recce troop commander, Captain Astley-Cooper. This modest force was to fight a valiant but tragic battle in the 8th Hussars' first Korean encounter with the enemy. (Private Collection)
78. During the night of 2/3 January 1951, the 29th Brigade was attacked in strength and both the Ulsters and Northumberlands were forced to give ground, but a counterattack by Cooper Force and the Churchills of C Squadron 7RTR restored the line, the Cromwells having fired every round of their ammunition. That night the brigade was ordered to withdraw through a valley along a track barely wide enough to carry the tanks which were to act as rearguard. As the troops fell back they were attacked at close quarters, but the fire of the tanks kept the enemy at bay until the infantry were clear of danger. Even so, the Ulster Battalion suffered 230 casualties in a battle which became known as 'Happy Valley', but had it not been for Cooper Force the final toll would have been far worse. Throughout the battle, in which he lost his life, Captain Astley-Cooper displayed conspicuous gallantry, and the photograph depicts his abandoned tank after the ground had been recaptured months later. (Private Collection)

78▼

▲79

79. While withdrawing through Seoul after the Happy Valley battle, one Churchill of C Squadron, 7RTR, struck a box mine and was disabled. It was blown apart by Royal Engineers to prevent it from falling into enemy hands. Note the hinged link for the Crocodile trailer on the rear hullplate in the centre of the wreckage. (Private Collection)

80. During the bitter winter of 1950–51, crews were quick to learn the problems of operating tanks in sub-zero temperatures. If the tank was parked overnight on muddy terrain it could become completely frozen to the ground by morning and attempts to extricate it under its own power would result in a burnt-out clutch or ruined final drives. Unorthodox methods to unfreeze tracks such as the use of hand grenades or lighted petrol proved hazardous, and it became standard procedure to park tanks on rice straw or ammunition containers to forestall the problem. (Private Collection)

▼80

81▲

81. Church parade is held in an A Squadron leaguer position; in the 8th Hussars, A Squadron is known as 'R Squadron' because of the supposed inability of Irishmen to pronounce the letter A. On the bazooka plate of the Centurion in the background is a shipping movement code, applied because of a War Office directive in early January whereby all Centurions were to be moved out of Korea. The order was countermanded within a week. (Private Collection)

82. During February 1951, the UN forces went over to the offensive and slowly but surely regained lost ground. The Churchill Bridgelayer proved its worth on many occasions, spanning cratered roads and destroyed bridges. On account of the limited forward vision in its travelling configuration, one enterprising 8th Hussars officer strapped a cavalry saddle to the top of the bridgelayer launching arm and thus could direct the driver from a much enhanced vantage point. (*Soldier*)

82▼

▲83

▲84 ▼85

83. On Sunday 11 February 1951, two C Squadron Centurions, 'Caughoo' and 'Colorado', commanded by Captain George Strachan and Lieutenant Mickey Radford respectively, motored up the road to Yongdongpo, an industrial suburb of Seoul on the south bank of the Han river. There they supported an American fighting patrol on the north bank, 'Caughoo' being the first Centurion to fire a shot in anger in any theatre of operations. Subsequently, a tank was observed under a bridge on a railway embankment. It was engaged and, at a range of 3,000yds, the second shot struck and destroyed the target which had been returning ineffectual fire with 75mm HE. It was identified as a Cromwell that had been captured and repaired after the Battle of Happy Valley. Further rounds started a fire in what appeared to be a petrol dump behind the Cromwell. For the next two hours the Centurions remained firing in support of the patrol, which at one stage was pinned down by a machine gun post. The position was quickly knocked out and the gun crew fled into a nearby house which was immediately hit by 20pdr HE and set on fire. The photograph shows 'Colorado' blasting away with 20pdr gunfire during the action of 11 February 1951. (*Soldier*)
84. Captain George Strachan MC (left) relaxes after the engagement in which his tank 'Caughoo' fired the first shot. (Private Collection)
85. The 20pdr main armament of 'Caughoo' is cleaned after the first tank-versus-tank battle fought by a Centurion, ironically against another British tank. (Private Collection)
86. 'Captain Cottle' lies in support of the Glosters during a Battalion attack on Hill 327 on 16 February when bunker after bunker was despatched with such accuracy that the action lasted only two hours from start to finish and became known, by virtue of its outcome, as Operation 'Copy Book'. 'SB' within a circle denotes a C Squadron Headquarters tank; in the turret were the regimental colonel, Sir William Lowther, C Squadron leader Major Henry Huth, and the squadron 2i/c Major George Strachan, who were observing the infantry attack through the 'times ten' peribinoculars while enjoying a bacon-and-egg breakfast. (*Soldier*)
87. The crew of the Universal Carrier 'Herald' relax after a meal break. The .50 calibre M2HB Browning was acquired from an American unit, and such weapons were mounted on many vehicles. The British were able to obtain many items through barter since they possessed a valuable currency in Scotch whisky and Asahi beer, American units being forbidden to have alcohol in the front lines. All vehicles in the Regimental Headquarters of 8KRIH began with the letter H, so 'Herald' was attached to RHQ. (National Army Museum)

86▲ 87▼

▲88

▲89 ▼90

88. B Squadron Centurions make a close leaguer with their turrets traversed outwards to form a ring of guns. The crews erect their 'bivvies' (bivouacs) on the lee of the tanks while drivers undertake essential maintenance. The 'S' within the square on the Centurion in the middle denotes the B Squadron leader's tank. (National Army Museum)

89. Centurions are repaired in a tank maintenance area behind the front lines. Despite being brand new on arrival in Korea, the Centurions of the 8th Hussars performed admirably; however, they did suffer a number of final drive failures, compounded by an incompatibility in the fit of spares made in different factories from those of the original manufacturers of the tanks. (Private Collection)

90. The rice paddy fields of Korea were a severe impediment to armour: in the wet season the soft glutinous beds made them impassable for tanks; in winter they were easily traversed but the frozen 'bunds' (raised borders to paddies) presented unscaleable obstacles. This Centurion Mk. III of B Squadron, 8KRIH, came to grief whilst testing the 'going' in an area of the Kimpo peninsula thought to be suitable for the employment of tanks. (National Army Museum)

91. A Churchill ARV Mk. II recovers the Centurion shown in the previous photograph. At the outset the Churchill ARV was the only vehicle with an effective winch but, owing to the age of the models used in Korea, it lacked power and was not very reliable. Its ability to tow a Centurion was limited because of its slowness, and it had difficulty steering on anything but hard tracks. Note the dummy gun fitted to this ARV to make it resemble a standard gun tank. (National Army Museum)
92. A Centurion Mk. III of A Squadron, 8KRIH, laden with troops of the 3rd Royal Australian Regiment, negotiates a pontoon bridge across the Imjin river. On more than one occasion the Centurion's ability to carry so many troops (the record being 56 in Korea) proved invaluable in moving infantry to and from the battle lines. (*Soldier*)
93. Men of the 1st Battalion, The Royal Ulster Rifles, advance northwards from the banks of the Han river with Centurions of the 8th Hussars in support during an operation to extend the Brigade front level. (*Soldier*)

91▲

92▲ 93▼

▲94 ▼95

96▲

94. The rough terrain north of the Imjin limited the penetration of the infantry fighting patrols, so armoured columns with infantry riding in the rear probed northwards up the wider valleys. On 20 April 'Lowther Force', comprising B Squadron, half of C Squadron, three Gunner OP Cromwells and two companies of Glosters, swept a series of valleys for the enemy, reaching eighteen miles into hostile territory. In one contact a group of Chinese was engaged and some forty men were killed. (*Soldier*)

95. An atmospheric shot of B Squadron, 8th Hussars, leaving the Imjin sector through the morning mist on 22 April 1951; it was replaced by C Squadron. At nine o'clock that night the Battle of the Imjin River began when the enemy attacked in overwhelming strength by the light of a full moon. (*Soldier*)

96. By the morning of the 23rd the enemy had crossed the river in great force and throughout the day the 29th Brigade forward infantry battalions, the Glosters, the Ulster Rifles, and the Belgian Battalion were heavily engaged by the 187th Division of the 63rd Army, 19th CCF Army Group. That night the Belgian Battalion, cut off north of the river, fought its way to safety. On the 24th the increasingly desperate plight of the Glosters, who had consolidated on Hill 235 repulsing regimental-sized attack after attack, dictated that every effort be made to relieve them. A counter-attack by half of C Squadron's Centurions and three Filipino M24 Chaffees attempted to clear the hills flanking both sides of the valley behind the Glosters. Unfortunately, the narrow, twisting road presented extreme difficulty to the Centurions and the advance foundered when the leading M24 was knocked out, blocking the road completely, and the column was forced to withdraw. The Glosters were now surrounded. The other half-squadron supported the Ulsters and Northumberland Fusiliers throughout the day; the tanks were in constant demand, invoked like guardian angels, at every point of threat and crisis. In the morning of the 25th, the Brigade was ordered to withdraw in the face of unrelenting enemy pressure, but after 72 hours of fighting the infantry were exhausted and barely able to walk. The withdrawal began smoothly under the covering guns of the 8th Hussars' Centurions and the 25pdrs of the 45th Field Regiment (RA), but waves of Chinese troops soon swept down from the hills and there was a real danger that all the tanks would be irrevocably cut off in the teeming cauldron of the valley. The Centurions were fighting in terrain totally unsuited to tanks, but they took extravagant toll of the swarming enemy. The Centurions surged down the valley, crushing enemy troops under their tracks. The firing was a continuous iron rain on the outside of the tanks and few of the infantry carried on their backs survived this death-ride. Inevitably, a number of tanks were lost to bazooka fire and bogging in the treacherous paddy fields but eventually the majority debouched from the valley and, momentarily, contact with the enemy was broken. However, a new crisis soon developed as wounded and desperately exhausted infantry were seen struggling down from the hills in an attempt to reach the road, just as a force of some 2,000 enemy was approaching. With only two Centurions at his disposal, Major Henry Huth, the squadron leader, moved forward to engage. In a brilliant and gallant rearguard action these two tanks were able to delay the Chinese advance, inflicting horrendous losses at every bound, until the infantry had reached safety. British casualties had been grievous by any standard: over a thousand men were lost in under three days fighting. Nothing had served to save the Glosters, but without the Centurions of the 8th Hussars the outcome would have been closer to the annihilation of the entire brigade. The photograph shows 'Three Bravo', Sergeant Cole's Centurion Mk. III, abandoned after shedding its tracks on leaving the mist-enshrouded road in the early morning of 25 April. The tank was blown up when it proved impossible to recover it during the course of the battle. (Private Collection)

▲97

97. 'Three Alpha', Sergeant Reekie's Centurion Mk. III, was knocked out by bazooka fire and sticky bombs, together with two Universal Carriers and a medical half-track, while fighting its way out of the valley. (Private Collection)

98. 'Four Bravo', Sergeant Holberton's Centurion Mk. III, was lost when his tank went head-first into a deep dyke and spiked its gun into the ground. (Private Collection)

99. South Koreans dig out 'Four Bravo'; the battlefield has been recaptured. Surprisingly, the Chinese made no attempt to retrieve the lost Centurions beyond burying their ammunition nearby and removing the pin-ups from inside the turrets. (Private Collection)

▼98 99▶

N
6

▲100 ▼101

100. Major Henry Huth in the turret of his Centurion 'Cameronian' in company with the CO and IO of the Belgian Battalion and, in the distinctive 'tent hat' of the 8th Hussars, the regimental liaison officer at Brigade HQ. Major Huth was awarded the DSO for gallantry during the battle. (Private Collection)
101. The 25th Canadian Infantry Brigade was supported by one squadron of Lord Strathcona's Horse (Royal Canadians) of the 2nd Armoured Regiment from May 1951. On arrival in Korea, Strathcona's Horse was equipped with Achilles 11C tank destroyers which were replaced by American 'Easy Eights' since the latter were more suitable for the fighting in Korea. An M4A3(76)W HVSS named 'Catherine' leads C Squadron, Lord Strathcona's Horse, along the banks of the Imjin as it moves up to the front lines. (Public Archives Canada)
102. After the Battle of the Imjin River, the Centurions were fitted with a .30 calibre Browning on the cupola ring on a mounting designed by the regimental technical officer, Lieutenant Micky Radford. After the 'human wave' attacks at close quarters during the battle, such a weapon was essential; some drivers welded a machine gun forward of their position but this was discouraged because they were required to concentrate on driving in the difficult Korean terrain. (US Army)
103. On 28 July 1951 all the British Commonwealth units in Korea were amalgamated under one unified command, becoming the 1st Commonwealth Division. The first large-scale divisional attack took place in October during Operation 'Commando', when I Corps moved forward to establish itself on Line Jamestown in order to deny to the enemy positions that they had prepared for either winter defences or offensive action. Here, an Australian officer observes as a Centurion Mk. III fires in support of the King's Shropshire Light Infantry in their successful attack on Point 355. (Australian War Memorial)
104. 'Cuddles', an M4A3(76)W mounting an M1 bulldozer, prepares a hill-top fire position for another tank of C Squadron, Lord Strathcona's Horse, during November 1951 as the 1st Commonwealth Division prepares a defensive line for the coming winter. (Public Archives Canada)

102▲

103▲ 104▼

▲105 ▼106

107▲

105. On 6 December 1951, the 8th King's Royal Irish Hussars were relieved by an equally famous cavalry regiment, the 5th Royal Inniskilling Dragoon Guards (5RIDG) – the 'Skins'. By this time the campaign had become static and the tanks were dug in on prepared fire positions atop commanding hill features. Here, a Centurion Mk. III of the Skins lies in a typical position during 1952. The scrim netting served no camouflage purpose since the enemy knew every tank position exactly, but it did act to mask the movements of tank crews entering, leaving or replenishing the tank, actions which if observed would receive unwelcome mortar fire in short order. (5RIDG)
106. 'Cougar', an M4A3(76)W HVSS of C Squadron, Lord Strathcona's Horse, keeps watch on the skyline as the crew of another Sherman, 'Camel', consume their C-rations on the reverse slope of a hill-top position. Note the underground living quarters of the crews beside the tanks. (Public Archives Canada)
107. Centurions of C Squadron, 1st Royal Tank Regiment (1RTR), ford the Imjin river. The Australian flag flying above the front trackguard suggests that one of the crew members was attached to 1RTR from the Royal Australian Armoured Corps. 1RTR took over from the Skins on 9 December 1952. (*Soldier*)
108. A Centurion Mk. III fires on a target during gunnery practice while the 1st Commonwealth Division is in reserve behind the lines during 1953. Note the powerful binoculars on the commander's cupola ring and the name 'Humourist' along the trackguard stowage bin. The name remains unchanged since the 8th Hussars' time as this is one of their RHQ tanks. (*Soldier*)

108▼

▲109

▲110 ▼111

109. At the beginning of April, the 1st Commonwealth Division returned to its previous sector of the front. As before, the squadrons in the line were deployed with just over half their tanks dug in on commanding hill features which were closely integrated in the infantry fire plan. Their tasks were to harass the enemy by day, destroying observation posts and defence works and preventing all daylight movement. By night they executed defensive fire plans (DFs) in the front of infantry positions to counter enemy raids or attacks, and fired prearranged shoots in support of friendly patrols in No Man's Land. The remainder of the tanks lay in reserve. Illustrated is a Centurion Mk. III on the extreme right-hand position of the Commonwealth front (which was actually located in the left-hand platoon position of the 1st ROK Division sector). (Private Collection)
110. A Centurion Mk. III dug in on Point 355, the highest feature on the Commonwealth front and a position known as 'Little Gibraltar'. (Private Collection)
111. This Centurion Mk. III occupies the right-hand half-troop position on Point 159. Note the crew's 'hootchie' or 'basha' (living quarters) dug in to the hillside to the right of the tank. (Private Collection)
112. Another Centurion Mk. III, this time on the left-hand half-troop position on Point 159. This was the 'hottest' tank position on the front, being on the end of a salient jutting out into No Man's Land and overlooked on three sides by Communist positions. (Private Collection)
113. Its 20pdr ammunition buried under a mound of earth and sandbags, a Centurion Mk. III rests atop a typical hill position. The sandbags on the glacis plate act as protection against mortar bombs. (Private Collection)
114. A Centurion Mk. III lies in wait for its next fire mission, its suspension protected by earthworks and dirt-filled ammunition containers. Note the .50 calibre Browning at the loader's hatches and the spare roadwheel at the rear to replace any damaged by shellfire. (Private Collection)

112▲

113▲ 114▼

▲115 ▼116

117▲

118▲

115. The blast of a 20pdr lights up the night sky as a Centurion Mk. III fires in support of a friendly patrol in No Man's Land. (Private Collection)
116. On the 25th Canadian Infantry Brigade's sector of the Commonwealth front, the Shermans of Lord Strathcona's Horse provided armour support from their perches on the highest peaks in forward infantry company localities. Although the infantry had an inherent dislike for tanks in their areas because they attracted heavy enemy fire, the close fire support that they provided both in defence and for offensive patrols was compensation enough. 'Cheetah', an M4A3(76)W HVSS Sherman, is shown here being prepared for action. Note the half-buried shell cases acting as switch markers for DF plans. (Public Archives Canada)
117. 'Carnoustie', a Centurion Mk. III of C Squadron, 1st Royal Tank Regiment, fords the Imjin river at speed. This particular Centurion is fitted with an armoured shield around the commander's cupola; it was designed by the Fighting Vehicles Research and Development Establishment following the experiences of the Imjin river battle but it proved unpopular because it made entry to and egress from the turret extremely difficult. (*Soldier*)
118. On the evening of 28 May 1953 the Chinese launched a major attack against the Hook salient which was held by the 1st Battalion, The Duke of Wellington's Regiment. Throughout the day all tank positions on the front line were subjected to heavy shelling by 122mm guns and mortars. In an attempt to destroy a tank, which they had failed to do to date, the Chinese excavated a bunker housing an 85mm anti-tank gun and engaged the Centurion Mk. III commanded by Lieutenant Mickey Farmer on the right-hand half-troop position on Point 159 (see illustration 111), but although the round struck the lower hull front it failed to penetrate. The tank was also hit by 122mm HE, knocking the 20pdr gun out of alignment and blowing off the commander's cupola hatch; the latter can be seen lying on the glacis plate forward of the driver's position. Although several Centurions had to be backloaded for repairs, none was knocked out by enemy fire in 1953. (Private Collection)

▲119

119. Australian troops unload heavy beams for the construction of front-line bunkers from a Centurion Tug, a battle-weary Centurion with its turret removed and used for supply tasks, for medical evacuation and as a tank retriever. (Australian War Memorial)
120. Brigadier M.P. Bogert, the commander of the 25th Canadian Infantry Brigade, inspects 'Calvados', an M4A3(76)W HVSS Sherman of C Squadron, Lord Strathcona's Horse, at its hill-top position. The tank is deployed in support of the 2nd Battalion, Royal 22e Régiment, the legendary 'Van Doos', whose ferocity in battle was possibly only matched by the Turks; both formations instilled abject terror into the Communists. (Public Archives Canada)

▼120

121▲

121. Tanks undergo maintenance and repair in Gloster Valley, the 'home' of 1st Royal Tank Regiment during their tour of duty in Korea. Note the two Centurions ARV Mk. 1; the vehicle in the foreground is having its engine changed by means of a Scammell Heavy Breakdown Tractor. (Private Collection)
122. The inadequacy of the ageing Churchills ARV Mk. II that were employed initially in Korea prompted the design of an ARV based on the chassis of the Centurion. The first models arrived in Korea in March 1952 and they fulfilled their recovery role admirably. This particular ARV served with C Squadron, 1RTR, and was commanded by Sergeant T. George of the Royal New Zealand Armoured Corps. (Private Collection)

122▼

▲123

▲124 ▼125

123. 'Beowulf', an 'Easy Eight' of B Squadron, Lord Strathcona's Horse, stands guard as troops bathe in the Imjin river. On the rear hull plate is welded a cradle carrying approximately forty 76mm rounds in their fibre cases. This device was fitted to several Canadian Shermans to augment the internal basic load when conducting prolonged fire missions. (Public Archives Canada)

124. Lieutenant-General Bruce Clark inspects a Centurion Mk. III of B Squadron, 1RTR, after the end of hostilities. A truce was signed at Panmunjom on 27 July 1953. In the background, with his idiosyncratic shepherd's staff, is Major General M.M. A-R-West, the commander of the 1st Commonwealth Division. (Private Collection)

125. A magnificent South Korean railway crane lifts a Centurion Mk. III on to a flatcar for backloading and transport to Hong Kong. In December 1953, 1RTR was relieved by the 5th Royal Tank Regiment, which remained in Korea guarding the uneasy peace for a year until all the tanks were withdrawn. (Australian War Memorial)